on the
FRINGE

Musings on Golf

by Brule MacDuff

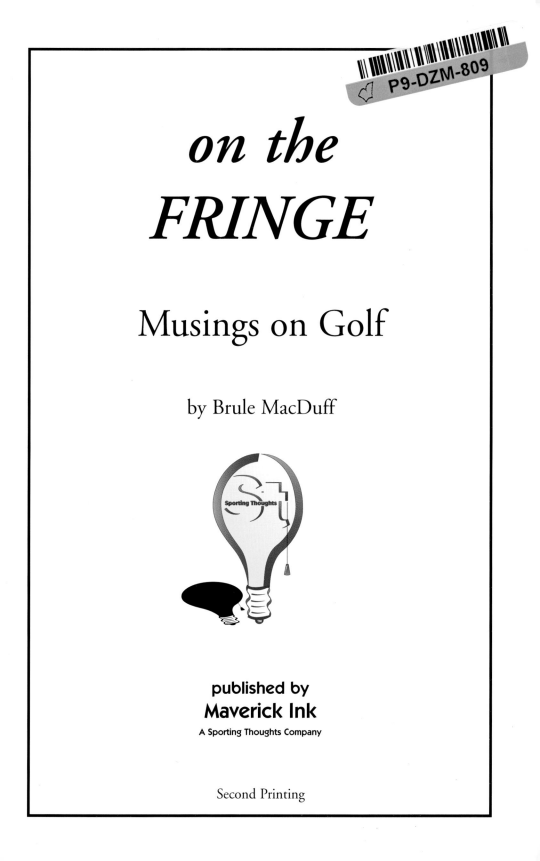

published by
Maverick Ink
A Sporting Thoughts Company

Second Printing

Some images used are protected by copyright. New Vision Technologies, Inc.;
Zedcor, Inc.; SoftKey International, Inc.; Sporting Thoughts
Some images used are original artwork by Joe Silver.
Cover design and illustration by Monte Cushman.

Written and Edited by Brad Closson aka Brule MacDuff

Second Printing

Printed in the United States of America

ISBN 0-9651096-0-7

on the Fringe is a product of *Sporting Thoughts*
11835 Roe Ave. Suite 244
Leawood, Kansas 66211-2607
(913)451-5700 ext.2
brule@sportingthoughts.com

To Meg MacDuff, for your love, patience, and encouragement. Your support and devotion to my writing and my affection for this game are both priceless.

I love you.

Contents

About this Book

About Brule MacDuff

Brule has been an avid golfer for over 15 years and has definitely been classified as a "golfaholic." Brule plays to whatever handicap he can get away with but is reasonably about a 5. He played both high school and college golf and had his own golf instruction business for 3 years. He has managed a golf range, taught college golf classes and coached high school golf. Brule has also worked at a golf equipment manufacturing plant and was the Director of Golf at a health club and spa. His many experiences with this crazy game have culminated in this book. He hopes you enjoy reading it as much as he did creating it.

Acknowledgments

As with most books, **on the Fringe** has been a team effort. Many people have helped to mold this book into the wonderful mass of mush that it is today.

Dawn Closson, Tom Reed, and Jim Closson were very helpful with their creative use of red ink (Ouch!). And a special thanks to my good friend Shawn Ashbaugh who has been instrumental in the layout, flow and editing of this literary masterpiece. His time, talent and friendship is much appreciated.

I would also like to acknowledge the artistic talents of Joe Silver, Monte Clark and Monte Cushman. Your genius with the pen and paper is a marvel. A special thanks as well to the skillful team at Colorworks. Paul, Jason and middle name Troy have been invaluable to this project.

Most importantly I would like to thank my partner and friend McReed, who has allowed this project to blossom and bloom. A Sporting Thought indeed.

Author's Note

Golf, my friends, is a game of honor, skill, and most of all, fun. It is a never ending adventure that is always different, always changing. A player can continually improve, and the enjoyment of this exciting contest can last a lifetime. Golf can be (well, "IS") cruel, exasperating, and at times humiliating, but it is a game that is meant to be enjoyed. I love this game. It makes me smile.........and cuss.

This book is meant to be a self-help guide and a handbook for better golfing. It is not, however, meant to be a divine work of art sent from a higher intelligence to heal your every golfing need. So if you see me on the street and I look just like any other shmoe, except more handsome, then realize that I am just a golfing legend in my own mind, or better put, a simple guy who knows a bit of golf, a bit of life, and a lot about looking silly on the golf course. So move onward my soon to be enlightened companions. It is time to "bite the bullet," or in more current verbiage, "load paper in the fax machine." Now, I must admit that "bite the bullet" has a much nicer ring to it, but both convey anguish and patience. You will experience ANGUISH, and you will need PATIENCE, so this rambling does have a point. Good luck! I did mention that I was more handsome than the average shmoe? Good. Just checking.

Brule MacDuff

The Game

Welcome

Welcome to "The Fringe." The fringe is a place that is close to the target, but not quite there. It's a spot to view the game and remind yourself that it's supposed to be fun. I take it that since you are reading this right now, you have not been playing golf long, or are wondering why you are still playing this funny game. You may possibly have a golfing event coming up in your future. Well, if any of these fit, then this little book should help you navigate the horror of a social or business golf outing. Some basics of golf, and a few of the important details of the game, are covered in this book. I realize, from experience, that the mere thought of playing golf in PUBLIC may cause you to have the chills or breakout into a cold sweat, but never fear, another quick-fix, band-aid, I-know-more-than-you book is here to save you. So hold on tight my curious friends because it's time to "cram" for that big, gut-wrenching test of life, the game of golf.

Introduction to Golf 101

To get things started on the right foot, let's take a moment to analyze our situation. Golf! What is it?

golf (gôlf, gôf) *n.* A game played on a large outdoor obstacle course having a series of nine or eighteen holes spaced far apart, the object being to propel a small ball with the use of a club into each hole with as few strokes as possible.
(American Heritage Dictionary)

This definition is lacking some of the vigor of golf. We need to add "a hideous, self-dissection of mind, soul and spirit, IN PUBLIC." Ahh, that's better. Let's move on.

Questions remain as to when and where golf really began. Though some say the Dutch first started swatting the ball as early as the 1300s, Golf is a game that most historians believe began in Scotland during the 1400s. "The gouf," as it was then called, was banned by King James II because it was becoming too popular and interfering with archery practice[1] Well, obviously the ban was not effective and golf has hung around until today. (But where's archery?)

The following poems may offer some evidence contrary to the popular belief that the Scots started golf. I was not there at the time, so I can only offer the exhibits and let you be the judge. Does this have anything to do with learning the golf game? No. But, information is power, and these rhymes are fun to recite anyway.

---

[1] History of Golf, by Michael Williams

Thorpar

Thorpar

Long before modern man,
when dinosaurs ruled the land
The first player was bunkered in the sand, Thorpar, of Golffa

Playing with clubs carved of bone,
and a ball of solid stone
His caddie was a hag named Joan, Thorpar, of Golffa

Overwhelming danger when he hit,
the bog, the lava, the great tar pit
Playing tag with a dinosaur,
and he's always "IT," Thorpar, of Golffa

So don't be fooled by history snots,
who claim it started with the Scots
A caveman hit the first golf shots, Thorpar, of Golffa

King Putt

King Putt

One last clink of the chisel, one last brush with the broom
Golf History would soon be re-written,
As the professor discovered the tomb

The air was thick in the ancient crypt, the dust was musty and deep
But his lantern lit up the tiny room, it was time to take a peep

He entered through this new found hole,
His heart quickened with every pace
For this was the vault of Egyptian lore, "Golf's first starting place"

And there it was, upon the wall, a painting of blue and red
This landscape told a story, and this is what it said.......

**"In the land of the pyramids, beside the shadow of the Sphinx
King Putt picked out his golfing staff, and headed to the links**

**Many holes are hazardous, the course borders on the Nile
You must avoid Cleopatra's barge, and of course the crocodiles**

**The sand traps they are many, for this game that Pharaohs play
The caddies all ride camels, and carve golf balls out of clay**

**Hook shots into Ra's backyard, a slice past Rameses palace
You better clear the mummy pit, or beware of archaic malice**

King Putt tapped in for his six, he was off to the last tee
This hole was his nemesis, much like crossing the Red Sea

He holed out from the fairway, what a shot for a birdie four
But a viper waited in the cup, Golf in Egypt was never more"

The professor stepped away in awe, for this story gave him chills
Golf was 30 centuries old, and was not from the Scotland hills

So let this be a lesson my friends, you must learn from this ancient verse
Golf is much more than a game, it is most probably a **curse**

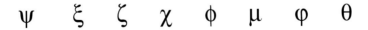

These poems may shed some light on the age-old question about where golf originated, or they may be a foul hoax written to confuse the poor golfing reader even further. Since the latter is almost impossible, I will only concede one thing. Golf is a curse, so hold onto your knickers because we're in for a wild ride.

The Golf Outing

You have been chosen by the boss or by fate or by your own naive self to participate in a golf outing of some sort. This may be a company tournament, a bachelor party, a date, or a client "shmooz" session. Anyway, the fact is as plain as the dry wheat bagel you had for breakfast, YOU are going to play golf! It's not going to be pretty, so let's not waste any more time.

EXCUSE ME!!! Have you lost your mind? Go back!! What are you thinking? This is the golfing jungle pilgrim, and I'm not sure you're ready for the test. Anyway, I'm the **Fringe Guide**, *and this is my partner* **Sport**. *It's our job to get you through this jumble of golf jargon. Stay loose, and be prepared for the unexpected. I know this MacDuff character, and he is really on the fringe, if you know what I mean. This golf outing bog reminds me of that time in the Florida everglades when I was trapped with…*

Where was I? Oh, the outing. So, you are heading off to play a game designed by the devil to give you a "taste" of Hell, and to, of course, have fun. Fine. We are all under a great deal of stress, so hitting a ball around in the wide outdoors should be a picnic compared to work, right? Well, read through this book, and you may survive this game which some call "a Scottish virus which infects the body, never to be cured!" Okay, that's just what *I* said, though others have said worse. So if you wish to take on this mission, proceed at your own risk.

The one that got away

As with fishermen, golfers tend to relate their skill to the ability of storytelling. It's the quality of the one that got away which marks the golfers competence. I am only relaying this to you, because I'm kind, generous, and in all honesty, I can't fish worth a lick, so I want to at least teach you how to tell a good golf story. Just remember these key phrases.

"It broke just at the end."

"If it had only kicked right."

"If I had made just a couple of putts."

"They top-dressed the greens."

"Man, we're talking WIND!"

"If it had carried one...more...foot!"

"And in the middle of my backswing....."

"If not for that spike-mark....."

The "Look"

Now, before we go any further, we need to get a few things straight. Golf is a game. Golf is fun. Golf is more exciting than it looks on television when you are clicking randomly through the channels, waiting for the next "real" program to start. Yes, to all of the above. But, the most important part of golf, for the "rookie" golfer, is "the look." (Do you hear bugles sounding?) This "look" is the presentation of the golfer to his/her peers — how he or she acts, talks, dresses, and of course, how this golfer accomplishes the task of "seeming" like a golfer.

The worst fear of every new person on the golf course is the "total nerd" syndrome. This is called *"hackaphobia."* Hackaphobia is the fear of looking, or even seeming, like someone who has no business at all being allowed on a golf course, let alone being outdoors without a leash. It is this impression of ignorance and lack of knowledge that has caused you to buy this book and is pushing you towards the next chapter. This fear is a sound one and is always present, so read on.

Dress Code

So it's time to get dressed for the big excursion. The key to adorning your body for this nature trek is to dress like a golfer, not like someone trying to dress like a golfer. I know this sounds a bit confusing, but look at it this way. If you were going sailing for the first time, you wouldn't get all decked out in an admiral uniform or a sailor suit. What you would do is wear comfortable clothes that wouldn't hamper your performance, yet would not make you stand out like someone trapped in the seventies wearing bell-bottomed overalls. (Yikes!) The same holds true with golfing attire. Many hackers shoot for the obvious — knickers, a visor, plaid pants, and of course, our favorite, polyester — all bad choices. These fashion tragedies will bring instant attention to your lack of golfing skill. Golfers wear comfortable, classy, outdoor clothes. They dress in layers and always have clothes that are color coordinated. A "new" golfer is judged as much on his/her outfit as he/she is on his/her ability. (Man, this politically correct "his/her" thing is wearing me out!) Look good, but don't be obnoxious.

These are a few rules to help you build your ensemble:

1)   Don't wear dress socks or dark shoes with shorts

I realize that your fathers have been known to wear dress socks and "church" shoes with shorts (painful flashbacks), but shorts are meant for white shoes (saddle shoes are allowed) and white socks. You have spent your lives being compared to your elders, here is a chance to be lumped into a new group, the fashion conscious.

2)   Wear golf shoes

This may seem obvious to you, but even "loafers" have shown up on the course. Golf shoes are a must. Period. Don't argue. Skip your lunch with Biff and go get some.

3)   Don't wear "lace protector" flaps on your shoes

Lace protectors are for those of you who wear pocket protectors and pull your pants up past your belly buttons. (No offense to Troy up on the third floor.) They are a direct emergency 911 call to the fashion police. Find some scissors and say "adios" to flaps of leather and lace.

4)   Don't wear a watch or obnoxious jewelry

Unless you are being paid a huge amount of money for endorsing a watch or jewelry product, stay away from them. Jewelry calls attention to you, and looking at your watch could make others think you have somewhere else more important to be, which of course you do, but that is beside the point. You want to blend into your surroundings. Camouflage yourself if you can. Don't signal the enemy!

5)   Don't wear sunglasses while playing

Yes, sunglasses are "cool." Yes, you will definitely wish you had a pair someday to hide your identity after you "hook" a shot into Ruth's back side, but golfers do not wear sunglasses while playing. Now it is Okay to wear them between shots if the sun is burning the moisture off your eyeballs, but sunglasses say, "I think I'm cool," "I think I'm something," "I'm probably more cool than you!" — all of which may express the wrong feelings towards your friends, your boss or, for heaven's sake, your date. So don't take your shades to the course, son, leave those shades at home, dear, don't take those shades to town.[2]

6)   Wear sunscreen

I won't go into that whole "CANCER, ozone, gamma-rays, death is coming" talk. I will, however, stress that everyone in the office did not get to take the afternoon off to play GOLF. So save that bronzed, golden, California tan, or that beet, lobster, ripe-apple burn for your vacation.

7)   Don't wear T-shirts or cut-offs

Golf is a game of style. As with any other endeavor, the better you look, the better you feel. Now, I'm not saying that cashmere slacks and silk shirts are on the menu, only that you shouldn't draw attention away from the other hackers. Do not announce that you do not have any respect for the game, which is what T-shirts and cut-off jeans say. Really! Well, they do not actually speak, but you get the picture.

---

[2]My Johnny Cash version.

8) Wear a golf glove

Not only is this the fashionable thing to do, but it will also protect your hand from blistering and keep clubs from flying out of your sweaty, slimy, greasy, grimy hands. By the way, you wear a golf glove on your left hand if you are right-handed, and vice-versa.
(DO NOT WEAR GLOVES ON BOTH HANDS. THIS IS NOT BOXING! THOUGH YOU MAY FEEL PLENTY BEAT UP AFTERWARDS.)

9) Wear a hat

A hat or cap takes away the usual stress of keeping your hair perfect. Remember, you are going to be outdoors (AHHH-HH), with no washrooms (EEEEEEE), no mirrors (ARRRGG), and subject to wind, rain, and passing birds (Sppplatttt). It may also protect your head from the heat and/or cold. I realize that you shampooed today, but on with the hat anyway.

10) Common sense

Basically, wear comfortable, neat, COTTON clothing.
(Yes, you can iron it, Christy!)   Avoid bright colors and "fashion statements." Golfers, obviously, have never been very concerned about fashion, so it is better to lean towards plain than towards "flashy." Melt into your surroundings. Wear earth colors. Okay already, enough said. Push on mighty golfing soldier, you have only just begun.

Equipment

*Ort need snake-
wedge....NOW!*

Now that we "look" good, it's time to head out to the garage or to the Golf shop and put together our equipment for the adventure in which we are about to partake. As with any activity, your equipment is a statement of knowledge.

Somehow it does not seem that impressive to see a rubber-headed hammer and two broken screwdrivers on a workbench. Conversely, (wow, that's a big word) seeing a Mark VIII all-in-one power center that can saw, hammer, grind, bevel, sand and compress old wood chips into ballerina figurines seems too much. The impressive workbench covers the bases. It has the right tools for the right jobs, and hopefully you can just sweep up the wood chips. There must be a good transition in there somewhere between wood chips and golf, but I can't see it. (Wood chips, wood, chop, hack, hacker. Okay, I have it now!)

Anyway, my long lost point is to look like you belong. Do not call attention to yourself by being naive about golf equipment. Follow these few guidelines and you will do fine. Well, "fine" may be a bit of a stretch, but you will survive, kinda.

1)   Always have club covers for your woods

Wood club covers are like the tie on a tuxedo. You don't have to wear it, but you are shouting "GEEK in the room" if you don't. Wood covers show that you respect your clubs and do not want them nicked by the constant contact with other clubs. So just because you bought your clubs in a garage sale doesn't mean you have to advertise the fact.(***Hint:** Avoid knitted pom-pon head covers. They look like your Grandma made them for you. No offense Dad.) You think Pom-pon is spelled wrong don't you? Look it up. You can use either spelling. HA!

2)   Always have at least 10 balls in your bag

"Why 10 balls?" you ask, "Why not 8 or 12 or 25?" There is not a set rule for carrying golf balls. Some of you may need 38. Ten is a nice number that usually covers normal hazards of play. One of the worst things that could happen would be to have to *borrow* golf balls from someone else by the 8th hole. If you work it right, you should always end up with more balls when you finish than when you started. Keep a keen eye out for them when *you* are in the woods, creeks and fields, and they will pop up everywhere.

3)   Toilet Paper (1 roll)

You will be hundreds of yards from bathrooms, washrooms, toilets....................well, you get the picture.

4)   Have a good bag

In everyday terms, this is like having nice clothes to cover your body. Yes, your body is important, but those clothes covering it are what everyone sees. Your bag will be noticed, even if your clubs are not.

Equipment......

5)   Have a GOLF umbrella

The umbrella will signify many things on the golf outing. It shows that you are prepared, responsible, and ready to do battle even in the rain. It might also help to shelter your boss, client, or co-worker who has been avoiding your advances.

I'm still working on our escape route. Sport believed he had an opening for you back on page 18, but he said it would be a tight squeeze. How can we get through this book unscathed? I was once tied to a runaway train, but that was with barbed wire, not golf jokes. And once while in Russia, I was lashed to the face of an ice cliff. But that was a different story because I had my retainer with me that time. That season in the South American rain forest when I was bound to a rubber tree with leather strips comes to mind. The natives had poured water on the hide, and as I struggled, the strips shrank. But I had a toothpick with me, so I'm not sure how it relates to this situation. Even with the strength of 5 men, which of course I possess, I will not be able to free us from this book with shear strength. A pity. Just stay calm and keep moving. I'll find a way out. The Fringe Guide always comes through. Like that time in Paris, 1968, when Sport and I were frozen in that block.....

6)   Boy Scout Kit

The "Boy Scout Kit" is a group of items that allows you to be ready for any situation. This kit should include band-aids, sun block, change for the pop machine or phone, extra tees, ball markers, pencils, lip balm, gum and your business cards. Taking five minutes to assemble these items into a freezer sack and popping it into your golf bag will be well worth the time. As with any endeavor, you want to be prepared for ANYTHING and EVERYTHING. Remember that if you forget it, you will need it.

7)   Avoid pagers and mobile phones

Yes, these accessories may make you "appear" busy, but during most situations, they are regarded as objectionable. (Brain surgeons and authors of golf books are exempt, of course.)

8)   Have plenty of golf tees

Don't be one of those tee-box combers who search the ground for lost and abandoned tees. Grab a handful from your loose change container on your dresser, look in the bottom of the washing machine, or dig out the barrel-O-tees that Uncle Ed gave you in 1979.

9)   Have good grips on your clubs

Make sure that you have good grips on your golf clubs before you embark on your escapade. Here is a quick quiz:

1. Does your club fly out of your hands when you are *not* mad?
2. Can you unwrap the leather strips off your driver?
3. Do your fingers fit into worn grooves?
4. Do you spit in your hand to get a better grip?
5. Have you watched the Olympics *twice* since you re-gripped last?

If you answered "yes" to any of the above questions, get some new grips. NOW!

10)   Carry some antacid tablets

Sand traps, doublebogeys, shanks, four-putts. Remember?

Your Hair

You didn't think Sport had a hair tip for you? This is a golf book, silly.

Move along!

The Language

Much more than a mere game, Golf is a culture, and as such, it has its own language. Now before we can venture deeper into this void that will suck you in quicker than you can say "double-bogey," we must learn about Golf's unique rhetoric. Many of these words and phrases are uncommon and rarely used in everyday life, so pay close attention to the following chapter so that you are not lost in the quick-sand of Golf babble.

Learning the "slang" is on *par* with being a *player*, so think not of your *handicap*, though a *hacker* you may be, and concentrate on *acing* this *round* of the game. (See what I mean? Try not to spit when you talk, Okay?)

Try this. The rain in Spain, falls mainly, on the plain. Good. Now try this. It's rain, that's plain, which is lame, but I came, to take aim, at this game, in my veins called GOLF. That's better! Onward my fair adventurer. Come master the words of Golf.

Vocabulary

As with any new endeavor, it is best to have a working relationship with the vocabulary involved. "Shop" talk is an important part of this game, and knowing it, as well as the facts, may (though I'm not promising anything) help you survive in the foreign land of the GOLF COURSE. The following is a listing of the basic terms you may encounter during your golf outing.

Ace
A hole-in-one. This is the dream shot of every golfer. If you get one during your outing, you will be a legend ....for life.
No one EVER forgets an ACE.

Adorning
Impressive big word which means "to clad" or clothe.
(Neat, huh?)

Ambivalence
The emotion felt on that last par three after you threw your clubs in the pond.

An Eight
Your usual score on a tough par four.

Another Eight
Your score on the easy par three following your first eight.

Approach
The shots that cause your ball to move near or nearer the green.

Away
As in "You are **AWAY.**" "Away" refers to the farthest position from the hole. When a golfer is away, it is her turn to hit.

Ball Marks
Indentations that are made on the green by the impact of the ball. These will be found predominantly between your ball and the hole when you are putting. Fix these little rascals if you are lucky enough to get them.

Banana Ball
A severe slice. When the ball veers impossibly right.
UGLY be thy name.

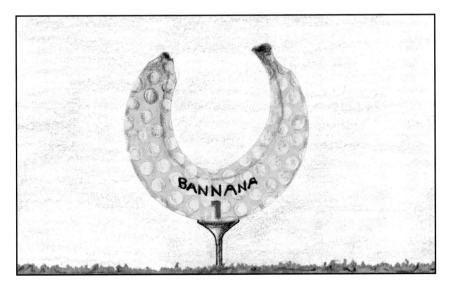

Vocabulary.....

Birdie

One under Par. If you are supposed to score a 4 on a hole and score a 3 instead, you shot a birdie. Birdies are nearly extinct.

Bogey

One over Par. If you are supposed to score a 3 on a hole and score a 4 instead, you shot a bogey. Golfers hunt for birdies but are hunted by bogeys!

Bunker

Another word for a sand-trap. Basically, a pit filled with sand that you want to avoid. Also known as "the beach."
(Can you say Frankie and Annette? I think you can.)

Card

A flat piece of stiff paper, usually rectangular, bearing significant numbers, yardage and rules. A diary of pain.

Carry

The distance a ball travels before landing. "My drive carried 250 yards!" (This is by air, not by pocket.)

Cheat

To deceive, mislead or fool. A fraud or swindle. A method used to break 80.

Chip

A shot towards the hole from just off the green. Also, a piece of tooth broken during an argument with your putter.

Vocabulary.....

Cup
The hole in the green in which the flag rests. The goal of golf, other than surviving in general, is to get your ball into the cup of each hole. The "pocket" in pasture pool.

Divot
Slice or pelt of earth dislodged by a hardy swing into the ground. A divot, or "scalp," is not a sign of power, so do not hook them to your belt.

Draw
The slight[3] movement of a ball in flight from right to left. The dream shot of most hackers.

Drive
Your first shot on each hole. (Usually followed by a swear word, an obscene gesture, or a mulligan.)

Driver
Wood or metal club with the #1 on the soleplate, used by golfers to hit the ball in strange and horrible ways. Known as the "torture" stick, this club will cause grown men to cry, women to swear, and children to duck.

---

[3]Gentle, tiny, soft. Not to be confused with SLICE.
Slight and SLICE have absolutely nothing in common. Get the picture?

Duck Hook

A mis-hit shot which bends sharply from right to left.
Whoa baby! Also described as a "Draw" on steroids.

This duck hook reminds me of that time in the Alaskan wilderness when I caught a polar bear using a golf tee and some dental floss. But that doesn't help us get through this book, now does it? Well, I still have to eat don't I? Bogeys taste like shoe leather and Eagles are on the endangered list, so get off my back. Move along Pilgrim. I'll catch up in a minute.

Eagle

Two under par. If you are supposed to score a 4 on a hole and shoot a 2 instead, you shot an eagle.
(Also known as a fluke of nature.)

EEEEIIIHHHHHHHHH!

The primal scream uttered by golfers when their new ball is headed for the center of the pond. This same scream can also be used when you are running naked in a snowstorm, being chased by an abominable snowman in heat, "EEEEIIIHHHHHHHHH!"

Vocabulary.....

Fairway
The closely mowed area between the tee and the green.
Rarely used.

Fast
Used to describe the players behind you. Never used for those snails that are always playing in front of you.

Fat
Word used to describe the action of catching too much turf (see Divot) while hitting your ball. Also called hitting it "heavy" or "catching the ball FAT."

Catching a ball "fat"

Five
The number of obscenities uttered after you four-putt.

Flag
Used to remind the golfers where to meet every 15 minutes.

Flashy
Something to wear to the disco or out jogging at night. Something that glows in the dark or could be seen on Oscar night. NOT something to wear to the golf course. It's not the 1970s anymore! (Whew!)

Forty
The number of yards your putter flies after the second four-putt.

"Golf, the final frontier!"

Vocabulary.....

Fore

Warning shouted at other players in danger of being hit by your ball. This phrase has the same affect as "Aunt coming" does at the family reunion. Those in danger cover their heads and hope for the best.

Gimmie

A very short putt which is given to you to speed up play. Watch out for golfers who take 5-foot gimmies; they are......cheating, yet are as common as houseflies.

Golf Cart

Golf's equivalent to the couch-potato's clicker. Vehicle used to avoid any resemblance of exercise or exertion.

Grenades

Just wanted to make sure you were paying attention. You may want one handy when Brad saves par from the parking lot to win a skin, but it would be better if you left them at home, Rambo.

Hacker

Most likely.... you. A hacker is a golfer who basically "hacks," "chops," or "flails" at the ball. If you hear this word whispered in your direction, smile and tell a joke. (Feel free to use one of the hilarious jokes found in this exceptional work of literature.)

Hand Wedge
The best club to get your ball out of a tough spot.

Handicap
The average score divided by the slope of the course rating, times the par value of ♉ minus the square root of the big dipper on polar opposite sides of a solar eclipse. Basically, your average score related to par.

Hazard
Bunkers, ponds, rivers, woods, lakes, ditches and port-o-potties. Things to avoid on the golf course.

Immediately
As in "Pronto" or "Right Now." How soon you must find a restroom after you eat that tasty protein bar.

Justice
Moral rightness, equity, fairness, due reward. Something *not* found in the game of golf.

Kick
Shot used to propel the ball from behind a tree back into the fairway. Also used to display anger towards your golf clubs lying innocently in the bag on the ground.

Vocabulary.....

Lie

Place where the ball comes to rest. If your ball comes to rest behind a tree, you have a bad lie. (Not to be confused with "Suzzane, I'm....*cough, cough*, sick today, *cough, cough,*, so reschedule, *cough, cough, sneeze, cough,* my presentation," which is a really bad lie.)

Through the green, past the sand, comes the tones of a jungle band.
The drums were loud, the beat was clear, a cry for help, a cry of fear.
A reader lost, no help in sight, jokes and stories he must fight.
Dread is rising, panic is near, the drums play on, for all to hear.
The Fringe Guide pounds into the night, a ray of hope at last in sight.
Don't be a afraid, my golfing friend, I am here until the end.
I'm off to scout, my true blue fans, but first I must go wash my hands.
These bones you see, they have a stink, so off I go to find a sink.

Ba-Ba-Boom. Later Pilgrim.

Line

The intended direction of your next shot or putt. (Not to be confused with the line, "What's a swinger like you doing on a course like this?")

Mulligan

"Hack #2, the sequel." Taking a second chance at a shot. Usually only allowed on the first tee box. Be careful, because you may catch "mulligitis," which is the sickness of constantly taking mulligans. Also known as "cheating like a dog."

Out of Bounds

Beyond the boundary of the course, which is usually marked by white stakes or a fence. Incur a two-stroke penalty if you find yourself here, unless the hand wedge or kick shot is available.

Par

The fictional score which you are supposed to get on a given hole. Yeah, right!

Penalty Stroke

A stroke added to a player's score according to the rules. For example, if you hit your ball into a lake, you incur a penalty stroke. (Do not confuse this with the Penalty "slap" which usually takes place in the back seat of your car. Skip over golfing and go straight to groping for more information about excessive strokes.)

Play Through

When a slower group allows a faster group to pass them on the golf course. Seldom happens.

Vocabulary.....

Player
As in "He's a player!" Refers to the fact that he can score more than two pars during one round and once made a birdie on a long par three. Wow!

Polyester
AHHHH! No, please no! The golfer's clothing curse. Good news, bad news. The good news is, "I have no wrinkles." The bad news is, "Yes, I'm a Brady Bunch geek who never learned how to iron."

Rapidly
Word often used to describe the approaching speed of a golf ball hit in your direction.

Rookie Golfer
An entrained recruit, a novice player, an inexperienced person. A BEGINNER, Okay? I was just trying to broaden my vocabulary. Crud lick.

Round
One rotation through the torture chamber, or what you owe everyone in the clubhouse if you get an "ACE."

Sadomasochism
Golf..........................in bed.

Scattered

Used to describe your foursome's drives, or how the group in front of you reacted to the word "Fore!"

Shank

A word that should never even be whispered. Shanking is a disease which affects the central golfing system. It is the act of hitting a ball at right angles of your target.

Shoot

A word used to cue your brain for an upcoming lie. "What did you <u>shoot</u>?" "Uhh, 82. Yeah, an 82."

Once I was playing on the coast of New Zealand when I hit my approach shot into........

Yeah, sure...

Vocabulary.....

Skin
What your hands lack after a hard day at the range. Also refers to the big-game-hunterish name for a bet on each hole. There's nothing like a 25 cent _skin,_ to get your juices flowing.

Skill
Something desperately needed on the golf course, yet scarcely found.

Slice
The sharp movement of the ball in flight from left to right.

Strange
Abnormal, odd, bizarre, irregular, unusual, well, you get the picture. Someone who golfs.........._a second time._

Stroke
One shot. How your score is counted. (You are still daydreaming about that Penalty Stroke comment, aren't you?)

Suck
A. To draw liquid into the mouth by inhalation. *B.* To golf... poorly. *C.* To make the ball dance on the green with excessive backspin. (Dream shot, so don't even fantasize. Stop it!)

Surprise
The feeling of wonderment and disbelief associated with making a par.

Tee
The wooden peg used to place your ball on when driving. Also used in the fairway by players with partners who are near-sighted.

Tee Box
Area where you begin your punishment on a hole.

Topped
Just catching the top half of the ball when you are swinging at it. Also called hitting it "thin."

Trehala
A sugarlike, edible substance obtained from the pupal case of a beetle. Really! Look it up.

A-PAR

So has MacDuff confused you completely yet? Well, I have a little story that Sport told me that may help you understand the magic of the game and at the same time, teach you some key words used in golf. It is the story of A-PAR, that mythical place where every golfer longs to be, but few find. This story brings to memory that time in the Outback when my faithful friend Sport was bitten by that scorpion. It was up to me to........

A-PAR
By Sport

It was a hot, steamy, summer afternoon as Cal brushed the sweat from his brow. The buzz of mosquitoes seemed to scream in his ears as he pushed his way through the dense overgrowth. He knew that his next move may bring an end to his entire mission, but still, he had one chance to survive.

It had been but moments ago when Cal and his group of adventurers had started this endeavor. They stood with weapons of steel, ready to transport their valued cargo to the promised land of A-PAR. Without warning, a group of nerves, called "jitters," attacked the small party. Cal was quick to engage the first wave but quickly fell beneath the swarm of fears. His implement of war misfired as he attempted to transport his payload. He watched in horror as the ivory treasure screamed out of control into the wilderness.

The ball beat like war-drums in the distance as it struck the thick walls of timber. Cal gave a great cry of despair and sheathed his club.

As with every linksman, Cal yearned for the promised land of A-PAR. Years of hard labor and pain spent on many barren ranges had given Cal the experience he needed for this quest, and he trudged on through the forest. Within minutes he found his prize, but as he surveyed his surroundings, he felt the hot breath of a BOGEY upon him. He fought back his urge to scream and tried to plan his escape from this wooden prison. Soon, though, he was surrounded by the images of BOGEYS, DOUBLE-BOGEYS, and suddenly, a SHANK.

His dilemma was soon evident. He could try a heroic charge at A-PAR, dueling the odds and tempting the scourge of a DOUBLE-BOGEY, by shooting straight for the green, green grass of home through a three-inch opening in the forest canopy OR he could do battle with a BOGEY right now, knowing that a bogey-bite would not scar him or bring down the fist of doubt upon his head. (That was hard to say in one sentence. Whew.... I'm worn out.)

There was no question in his mind. Cal was a golfer. He was brave, he was proud, he was, as most golfers are....................... a fool. He pulled his club, and without hesitation, sent the ball towards its haven. The snowy orb shot straight and true, avoiding lumber, Shanks, and even a menacing beach of sand. Cal would find the warmth and embrace of A-PAR. It was like a drug, and soon he was off, searching once more for the prize, A-PAR.

As he strode towards his next adventure, he could not help hear the whispers of the evil ones mocking him from the forest. "We will be waiting," they growled, "and your scalp will hang from a DOUBLE-BOGEY'S belt." "We will wait for you................... we will **NEVER GO AWAY!**"

Cal smiled. He still carried the old scars from wounds past, but his skin was tough, and he was ready to do battle again.

Beware of BOGEYS

On the road to A-PAR

Interpretation

Another basic fundamental that you may need to know on your golf outing is INTERPRETATION. This section of the book will help you decipher some of the golf "gibberish" that may be flying left and right on the course.

Phrase or statement	INTERPRETATION
"Never up, never in"	Don't be short on that putt, you fool.
"Golf is 90% mental, 10% physical"	You need a better attitude, because your swing stinks.
"Drive for show, putt for dough"	Long drives look great, but putting is how you score.

Phrase or statement	INTERPRETATION

"You're fired"

You should not have beaten me today.

"Nice shot... from there"

Polite way of saying..
"That shot was worthless, but you must have been in a tough spot."

"&*%^$#@^%$&*"

Darn it. Shoot. Dang. Phooey. Raspberries. Most common words spoken on a golf course. (Actually, the ugly cousins of the above words.)

"It's just a game"

This phrase is spoken to you by another when you just hit the worst shot of the day, pulled a clump of hair out, and lost your last ball. Your best replyis...."Stick it!" Just kidding. Actually, you should reply......
"Oh, boy, the fun, the fun!"

It's just a game!!

"Your honor"	You hit first, you lucky skunk.
"Things could be worse"	"Quit being a baby, it's just a game, so buck up little camper."

Sand wedge again, McReed?

"I think that ball is OB!"	Grab another ball. You won't find that one.
"Bite"	Darn, I hit it too far.

"Sit down"	BITE!
"Here, I found it"	I dropped a new one out of my pocket.
"Fore!!"	Think fast!!!!!
"Great putt!"	Man, are you lucky.
"Good Shot!"	You really make me sick!

When lining up your fourth putt.......

The Basics

The "basics" are like the rules you learn during your first day of orientation at a new job. It is important that you go over them, though most of the other folks do not pay any attention to them anyway. We do, however, need to have a foundation to build upon for our golf excursion. Knowing these simple basics will help you become a better person and enjoy yourself more on the golf outing. (Boy, what a crock of creamed corn.)

The Swing

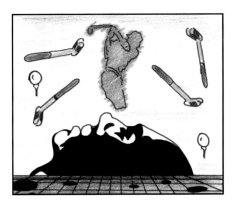

Okay, things are desperate. Your eyebrows have finally grown together. It's time to get out the tweezers and...........oh, sorry, wrong chapter. Where was I? Oh, yeah. You don't have much time before your golf outing, and you need a couple of swing tips to get you started. Well, this is not the place to look. You need a lesson my friend, either from a buddy, or better yet, a golf pro. I'm not going to waste your time or mine by trying to explain how to swing a golf club. I will, however, give you a few basic swing hints.

The Swing.....

Swing Thoughts:

Make sure your weight is evenly distributed on each foot. Keep your back straight, your knees bent, your head still, your muscles relaxed and your mind clear. Better yet, leave your weight on your back foot, keep your knees straight, tense up and think about everything you are doing wrong. That way, you will look like every other golfer on the course.

Pose:

Hold a great pose when you hit a good shot. It could be weeks, months or even years before you hit another good shot, so wallow in the moment.

Warm Up:

Make sure you stretch out before you hit, or play, or........swing. It will also help to warm up your mental state. A swift blow to your shin with an eight iron will prepare your mind for the anguish to come.

(If you are playing for money, make sure to hit both shins.)

Keep Your Head Down:

Keep your head down. Keep your head down. *Keep your head down!* Did I mention to keep your head down? And don't forget to keep your head down. Don't make me get out that twine and hay hook. (Ouch!)

Practice Swing:

Use your "real" swing when practicing and your practice swing when you hit. Pretend the TV analysts are critiquing your fine finish. "Look at that follow through, Gary. The grace, the beauty, the style. He must have heaved that club 75 yards."

Swingers:

Avoid the line, "What is your sign?" and beware of who you "play a round" with.

The Swing.....

❖   ❖   ❖

Focus:

Keep your eye on the ball, your mind on the target and your TV clicker handy. Now when you are **playing**, focus on the quality of the swear word you are about to mutter.

❖   ❖   ❖

Swing Key:

It is best to think of one swing key before you hit. "Keep my elbow in" or "Grip pressure light, muscles relaxed" or "Point my back at the target, then release." Avoid such swing keys as "Should I get a hot-dog or a candybar at the turn?" or "These socks don't match at all" or "I'm worthless and don't deserve to live, let alone play this game which is killing me, and I know I am going to hit it out-of-bounds or in the water and..........."
I think you get the picture.

❖   ❖   ❖

Etiquette

Now as Brule's father, it is my duty to tell you folks about the etiquette of this game. Now section 7 of part three from the paragraph in rule 94 of the etiquette code states that "a good son will always mention his father during the course of his book." This will do son. On with your work.

Golf is a very structured, rule-oriented game. It is a game of honor and pride; thus, it has a strict guide of etiquette that must be followed. Now, being "politically correct" is the big fad of today, but on the golf course during your outing, it is best to be "etiquettely correct." The following section will briefly update you on the code of behavior expected on the links. Follow this code precisely, you heathen, or suffer the fate of "faux pas." (That's FO-PAW for you commoners.)

❋ ❋ ❋

Do not distract other players while they are hitting. No talking, yelling, squealing like a pig, or smacking your gum, Homer.

Etiquette.....

* * *

Always rake the bunker after you hit. The sand traps are already a prison sentence without having to play out of a footprint.

* * *

Do not walk in your playing partner's line before he putts, even if he _is_ your brother.
(Well, unless he is your _younger_ brother.)

* * *

Do not drag your feet on the green. Putting is a chore in itself without trying to maneuver through spike trenches. Walk gently. Pretend you are carrying a glass of grape juice across your mother's "roped off" living room. If you snag that foot, you can always blame your brother, but _someone_ will feel the wrath of MOM. If your mom were the greenskeeper, you would NOT drag your feet. Compréende?

* * *

* ❋ * ❋ * ❋

Avoid slow play, excess practice swings, working overtime, practicing on the green and hitting your ball into a mosquito-infested bog.

* ❋ * ❋ * ❋

Allow faster players to "Play through."   If you find that everyone is faster than you, then PLEASE QUIT THIS GAME AT ONCE!

* ❋ * ❋ * ❋

The really early tee-off time.

Fix your ball marks! Next week that gouge may be in *your* line.

Etiquette.....

* * *

Use a ball marker or coin to mark your ball on the green. Do not use a twig, leaf, or gold bar from a James Bond movie.

* * *

Be considerate of the other golfers playing the course. They were foolish enough to spend $35 dollars to play, just as you were.

* * *

Replace your divots on the fairway *and* the green.

* * *

Do not dance naked down the fairway when you make a 48-foot putt for bogey. Save it for birdies.

Rules

McReed at Work

We do not have the time, or the need, to go into all the rules of golf. As with any game, there are many rules and regulations, but you will pick them up, or make them up, as you go. During the Golf Outing, you will not be expected to know ALL the rules, but knowing a few key ones will help you get through your day. Remember, however, that you can always ask someone else about the rules. They will lie to you, or offer some far-out "local" rule, but you can always ask. You will not be tested over this material, but it may give you a better understanding of this crazy game.

Count every stroke

This rule is bent, twisted, and broken more than any other, but since this is a game of honor, you need to count every.......single.......shot. (Remember, every swing is a shot, even if you miss the ball.) Calculators are allowed.

Rules.....

No cheating

Do not move the ball to a better spot, kick the ball from under a tree, forget the correct amount of strokes, or use the eraser in a malicious manner while others are watching. Wait until your partner has his back to you.

Take the correct penalty strokes

Water hazards are one stroke, and out-of-bounds are two strokes. Your wife being paired with your girlfriend on ladies' day is a massive stroke.

Have fun

This is not an actual rule, but it should be. You are not in the office, at the Department of Motor Vehicles, or in traffic. You are in the great outdoors, playing a game, so do it AND LIKE IT!!!!!

Advancement

The only way to advance the ball in golf is by using a club. You may not throw, kick or nudge the ball, unless you are a scoundrel, which entitles you to break all of the above rules.

"You stepped on Sport's ball AGAIN!"

Basic Do's and Don'ts

I thought it might be useful to throw out a few basic "do's and don'ts." We have covered the main principles of the game, including etiquette, rules and the swing. This next section will give you a shotgun blast of other helpful tips. These hints will help you steer through your golf jaunt. Read these carefully, and don't forget to floss.

❖   ❖   ❖

Don't bet with players who might.......*beat you.*

❖   ❖   ❖

✤　✤　✤

Do call ahead for a tee time.

✤　✤　✤

Don't use the same swear word twice in one sentence.
It shows a lack of creativity.

✤　✤　✤

Do eat a balanced breakfast, including all four food groups.
(Coffee, pork, butter, and donuts)

✤　✤　✤

Don't use shag balls[4] for water hazards. Be confident. Be
strong. Be the ball. (Fine, use the shag you wimp!)

---

[4] Old balls which are cut, out of round, or X'ed out. The ones our Dads use

Basic Do's and Don'ts.....

✤   ✤   ✤

Do brush after every meal.

✤   ✤   ✤

Don't use mulligans more than once. No trulligans please.

✤   ✤   ✤

Do play quickly.

✤   ✤   ✤

**Don't tee the ball up in the fairway
unless no one is watching, duh!**

✤   ✤   ✤

❖   ❖   ❖

**Do have a good excuse ready when you hear the sound
of breaking glass.**

Don't believe in shortcuts on the golf course.

❖   ❖   ❖

**Do yell "Fore" if your ball is heading for another group,
unless it is the third time today you have hit into that group.
In that case, just run.**

Basic Do's and Don'ts.....

❖   ❖   ❖

Don't throw your clubs unless you throw them in front of you. That way you do not have to walk too far out of the way.

❖   ❖   ❖

Do say "Nice shot," when others hit a good one.
(Or just spit in their direction
if you don't like them.)

❖   ❖   ❖

Don't think about more than 136 different key thoughts during your swing.

❖   ❖   ❖

Do be careful of too many practice rounds.................at the bar.

Danger - Danger

*Did I hear the word "Danger?" I thought so. How have you been pilgrim? You made it this far, which is impressive. I've been out searching for Sport. He got lost back in the Rules somewhere, and I had to rescue him from a pack of golf-hating wives. It was not a pretty sight. It reminded me of that time I had to fight off a pack of Werewolves in the Gypsy village of Blama, just north of the French border. They had me trapped in an old mine shaft and were quickly moving in for the kill. Well, to make a long story short, I saved my life with a rock, some fillings and a high heeled shoe. **Don't even ask.** My point is that "danger" is just in your mind. Don't let this MacDuff character scare you off. What kind of name is "Brule" anyway? Let me tell you a story about real danger. My good friend Shawn was on this island......*

Shawn was stranded on a desert island. He hadn't had a drink or a bite to eat for 14 days. One afternoon, as he was climbing a palm tree in search of coconut beetles, he spotted a diver approaching the island. In his haste to signal the diver, he fell from the tree. When he awoke, a young woman, in a skin-tight wet suit, was standing before him.

"Water," he faintly whispered. "Water."

The young woman unzipped a compartment in her wet-suit leggings and pulled out a flask of water. Shawn drank it rapidly.

"Food?" he asked, questioningly.

She then unzipped a compartment on her waist and retrieved an entire roast duck. He stared in amazement, wondering where these things came from.

"Smoke," he quibbed, almost jokingly.

The young lady smiled and pulled a box of cigars from a pocket in her swimming gloves. She then turned to Shawn and with a smile she began unzipping her wet-suit top.

"Do you want to play around?" she asked raising her eyebrows.

"YOU HAVE GOLF CLUBS IN THERE TOO?" Shawn shouted.

Back to the Danger. Don't make me tell you again!

Contrary to popular belief, golf is a dangerous sport. Golf is made up of hunting for birds, avoiding hazards, fighting the weather, defending your honor, and beating things with a stick. Danger abounds on the golf course, and you should be aware of these liabilities.

Obvious Danger

Obvious danger is........well.........obvious. It is the type of danger that jumps right out at you and really makes you feel STUPID when you ignore it. Use your common sense. You know, that thing which you ignored when you took up golf.

Don't stand near the swinging golfer.
This statement could be compared with...
"Don't run into the boss on your SICK day."
Obvious, yet still broken.

Don't wander in front of the practice range,
even if your insurance *is* up to date.

Don't drink with the devil.

"Let me get this straight. My Golfing soul against eternal life, wealth beyond my dreams and golfing every day with the skill of Greg Norman? What's your handicap again?"

❈   ❈   ❈

Don't play in lightning storms. You are anchored to the earth with METAL SPIKES and swinging METAL RODS.
Think about it.

❈   ❈   ❈

Don't race the golf carts...
well, unless you have a chance to win.

❊　　❊　　❊

Don't have a club in your hand, when you get mad. If a fit of
anger overtakes you, throw down that horrible golf cap you
are wearing and stomp on it.

Please.

❊　　❊　　❊

Don't ask for a lesson if the pro has the "shanks."

Island Greens

Subtle Danger

Subtle danger is the type of jeopardy which may catch you off guard. You need to pay a bit more attention than you did in 7th grade sppellllling to catch this peril. Be aware, be ready, and evil spirits "be GONE!"

When the Fringe Guide told me not to go left, he was really serious. "Don't go left! Don't go left!" Of course McReed was right there telling me, "Go for it Jason. No trouble over there." Where's that 50 foot ball retriever when you need it?

Beginners with graphite shafts in their clubs. Graphite tends not to bend, if you get the picture.

Subtle Danger.....

A golfer who yells "FORE," shoots a six,
and writes down a five.

✳   ✳   ✳

One lone rain cloud when you are teeing off.

✳   ✳   ✳

Someone spotted reading *this* book
before they head to the course.

✳   ✳   ✳

Finding your spouse's clubs in the closet
when she said she was "out golfing."

✳   ✳   ✳

Attempting to teach someone else how to play golf.

Washing your ball before a water hole.

Trying NOT to hit the ball into a hazard.

Skipping your yard work to play golf when your wife knows voodoo.

*"So, you are going golfing instead of mowing the lawn? **FINE!**"*

Subtle Danger.....

Thinking that you have this game whipped.

GOD and Jesus were playing a round of golf. On the fifteenth tee, a long par 3 over water, Jesus had the honor.

"What are you hitting son?" asked GOD.

"Arnold Palmer hit a 7 iron here, and so will I," Jesus replied.

He took a mighty swing at the ball and watched as it came up 30 yards short into the lake.

"If Arnold hits a 7 iron, then I can too," Jesus cried, teeing up another ball. It too fell short into the water.

As he was digging in his bag for a third ball, GOD teed off. His ball skipped twice across the water, bounced off a turtle's back, was picked up by a squirrel and deposited into the hole.

"Show-off," Jesus muttered.

"You should use your 5 iron son," GOD spoke gently.

"If Palmer can do it............." He did not finish as his ball land-ed in the water. Since he was out of balls, he set out walking across the lake to retrieve one.

A passing greenskeeper spotted him and yelled, "Who does he think he is.....Jesus Christ?"

"No," smiled GOD. "He thinks he is Arnold Palmer."

Golf Outing Laws

Golf Outing Laws are like the "laws of nature" or the "laws of the jungle." They cannot be explained, yet it is important that you are aware of them before you venture into the realm of the golf course. The following section will give you a brief list of a few of these laws. You will soon get the idea.

※　　※　　※　　※　　※

Most great shots will be followed by two cruddy ones. The sad thing is that most cruddy shots will be followed by three more cruddier (good word, huh?) shots.

※　　※　　※　　※　　※

Golf Outing Laws.....

The harder you try to lose to your client,
the better you will play.

❖ ❖ ❖ ❖ ❖

Your boss is allowed an extra club, the "hand wedge."

❖ ❖ ❖ ❖ ❖

The higher your score is on a hole,
the more likely you are to make the putt.
That 27-foot putt for an eight always goes in.

❖ ❖ ❖ ❖ ❖

The farthest point from shelter
has the highest chance for rain.

❖ ❖ ❖ ❖ ❖

It is easier to hit a one-inch twig than
a 100-yard-wide fairway.

❈　　❈　　❈　　❈　　❈

No matter how bad things *seem* when you are playing,
they can ALWAYS get worse.

❈　　❈　　❈　　❈　　❈

That tree which is "90% air" will stop your ball 90%
of the time.

Golf Outing Laws.....

You will forget your sun screen
the day you are skipping work.

⁂   ⁂   ⁂   ⁂   ⁂

Your bad shots will be witnessed;
your good ones will be missed.

⁂   ⁂   ⁂   ⁂   ⁂

Your ball will travel the farthest
when hit in the wrong direction.

⁂   ⁂   ⁂   ⁂   ⁂

Rotten luck can only be passed on; it cannot be lost.
Remember that if one part of your game is working, another
part is ready to BRING YOU TO YOUR KNEES. Sorry, it's a
fact. Good putting, poor driving........Good driving,
poor chipping....
...Good golly, Miss Molly........

If you are playing a new course, your partner will say, "Did I forget to mention that those blue stakes are out-of-bounds?"

Well, pilgrim, it seems that our host Mr. MacDuff is not too happy with the Fringe Guide. No need to fret though, because I have him right where I want him. He thinks that you can go it alone from here on out, but don't you worry my golfing friend, because I'll be waiting at the end for you. You know, this situation reminds me of that time at St. Andrews when Sport and I were caught sneaking......

Those good shots you hit on the range.........
................were flukes.

One "I hit that perfect" will erase ten of "I hate this game"

The greatest distance between two points on the golf course is the space between the clubhouse and your broken down cart.

You will start to hear voices in your head, and they will be whispering, "Miss it!"

You will always lose new balls, but you can never get rid of that cut one in the bottom of the bag.

The older you get, the richer your chiropractor becomes.

Saturday's will ALWAYS be a battle.

One More Saturday

Twas the night before golf, and there was so much to do
All the chores must be finished, all one hundred and two

The queen of this castle, had made it quite clear
"All these jobs must be finished," so he mumbled, "Yes, dear"

He looked the list over, from his throat came a groan
"But my tee time's at 8:00," he said with a moan

"Here's your choice, plain and simple," she said with true glee
"Chores now, golf tomorrow, Or come shopping with me"

Woe is me, oh the pain, he thought with real fright
I will never go shopping, I'll put up a fight

Golf is my life, and some call me a nut
But it's worth all this anguish, for a chance to three-putt

So he started to work, thinking only of pars
He would work until midnight, by the light of the stars

Re-stack the soup cans, clean the sink traps
Level all the pictures, fold the car maps

Spackle the ceilings, clean the leaves from the gutter
Change all the spark plugs, the boat needs a rudder

He picked up his mop, then reached for his broom
"I must defrost the freezer, and paint every room"

The floors would be cleaned, so don't call him a liar
He swept under the washer, not to mention the dryer

The attic was scrubbed, from the rafters with care
Cause somehow he knew, that SHE would check there

He cranked up the mower, found the spray for the bugs
Put the storm windows on, and vacuumed the rugs

And the Christmas lights too, once he cleaned that grease stain
Will he find that loose bulb, or just go insane?

When what to his horrified eyes, did appear
But a fingerprint smudge, on the main bathroom mirror!

To his lips came a grimace, but his eyes had that gleam
He called to his crew, gave a shout to his team

"On Comet, on Pine-Sol, on Clorox, and Car Wax"
"On Spic and On Span, 409 and Ajax"

"To the bathroom with speed, to the smear with all haste"
"My wife will be checking, there is no time to waste!"

Yes, bogeys are painful, and four-putts are mean
But real **FEAR** is SHOPPING, he would much rather clean

At last he was finished, so glad to be done
He could golf and not shop, one more Saturday was won

The Fears of Golf

The Fear

Every new venture that we face in life has its share of fears involved. Golf is no exception. The whole "fear" family lives close to the golf course. Danger, pain, disaster, terror, and even cousin dread are all common feelings felt each and every day by the golfing public. Fear is a sneaky little monster that lurks in the shadows of every shot, and can cling to you like your little brother at the store. Many fears, however, can be calmed if you know what to expect in advance. This section will point out some of the major FEARS associated with golf.

What to hit

Golf today is made up of many decisions. You need to decide what to wear, where to play, who to play with, what "sick" lie to give the boss and most obvious, what to hit. How far do you hit your seven iron? Your seven wood? Do you hit more club on an uphill lie, or less club on a side-hill lie? This fear is real and will remain with you until, basically, you die, or quit playing. So the best thing you can do is say this special word, which always makes me feel better.

Super-para-fromthe-rougha-expialladocious

(Just don't say it out loud. People will talk.)

Wood or Metal?
White or Blue Tees?
Steel or Graphite?
Blade or Cavity-back?
Cord or Wrapped?

Man, I need an aspirin! Where's that
Fringe guy when you need him?

The Course will be too tough

This is a *game* folks. Don't worry about how hard the course is. Yes, you will lose hundreds of balls. Yes, you could lose a friend, and even your life. But the key is not to show your yellow-bellied, spineless, wet-palm, chicken-livered cowardice to the public. Have some dignity. Fear is your friend on the golf course. Well, not really your friend, but more like a hated neighbor who never mows and has a garage sale every Saturday. You wish this horrid thing would die, but you live with it anyway. So quit whining. Pleeeeeease!

"FORE!!"
Sport needs to learn that "fore" is not a number, it is an alarm.

Forget that I mentioned this fear. It falls into the "reality stinks" category and is one that will never go away. Years of therapy and a number of shock treatments have not helped me block this consternation. (See, I even use big, blow-hard words to describe it.) Just do the best you can. The course is there to scare you.

BOO! (Just testing you.)

The Water Hole

I stand and stare with ball in hand
A silent prayer that I'll hit land

The water looms, I feel the horror
I make a wish for the other shore

So many yards my ball must fly
I tee it up, with a final sigh

My heart stands still, I cannot hide
Then one last look to the other side

My breath, it now comes hard to me
The pond has turned into a sea

Psst. Hey, over here. Shhh. I'm still with you pilgrim. I've been making my way through the lines to find you. I'm cold and wet and hungry, but I'm still on the job. This adventure reminds me of the time that I was lost in an underwater cave off the coast of Cuba. I was trapped under a 27 foot shark, which I had just subdued using some toenail clippers and a band-aid. Well, it was just my luck that....

My vision blurs, my muscles shake
The sweat beads pour, my ankles ache

The hazard seems to call my name
I curse the day I found this game

At last my swing, a strong release
I bid farewell and "rest in peace"

I cannot watch, my eyes held tight
But I hear no splash, could this be right?

I can't believe my very eyes
My rash is gone, my cramps subside

For yonder on the distant bank
Lies my ball which never sank

I smile and wink at my golfing group
My ball is safe, not in the soup

I can't forget though on this day
One water hole down, but six to play

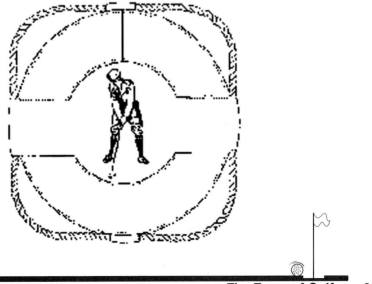

Mind Games

Fancy meeting you here pilgrim. I just wanted to check in with you. Hope things are going Okay. Don't let this Brule fellow catch you off guard. Yeah, he may be funny, but ouch, but ouch, ouch! Darn cobras. Sorry, I need to move right away. Later!

Another thing that some of us fear is the mind game. This is also called gamesmanship. It is often used by players to gain an advantage but can also be used in fun. Try out some of these mind games on your partners...if it is appropriate. And be ready for some of the same from them.

"Do you breath in or out on your backswing?"

"Be careful not to SHANK!"

"I can't remember the last time you three-putted."

"That out-of-bounds is just jumping out at us."

"Do you have enough club to clear THAT hazard?"

"Whatever you do, DON'T BE SHORT!"

"Do you always grip it like that?"

The Pain

The pain, oh, the pain..................................

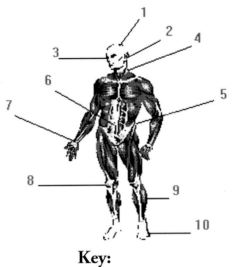

Key:

1) **Headache** - Caused by the stress of adding up your score without a calculator.

2) **Earache** - Caused by listening to your own shrieks of anguish on the course.

3) **Sore eyes** - Caused by watching your own shots all day long. Ouch!!!!

4) **Pain in the Neck** - Caused by your partner, whose new phrase every time he tees it up is: "It's time to pee in the tall grass with the big dogs."

5) **Lower back pain** - Caused by that "Big Dog" swing you took yourself on #4, after topping it on #3.

6) **Stomachache** - Caused, of course, by those chili dogs at the turn.

7) **Sore wrist** - Caused by the excess use of your "hand wedge" to get out of the trees.

8) **Knee strain** - Caused by trying to jump over that stream on #14. You are not 12 anymore. Hello!

9) **Calf pain** - Caused by that 3rd degree sun burn. "Sun block? Naw, I'll be fine."

10) **Sore feet** - Caused by those new $125 shoes. They sure look good though

Bad Luck

It's bad luck to fear bad luck, though that is a type of double negative, so maybe that is good luck. I doubt it. Bad luck is the foundation of golf. Without it, you would have no luck at all.

Big Mistake!

Just when you thought things could not get worse!

The good thing about bad luck is that you can blame it for everything. It's bad luck that they put a pond right there, and it's bad luck that your elbow keeps flying right, and it's bad luck that you happened upon that new Superduperextralong driver, which you can't hit out of your shadow. That darn bad luck seems to be everywhere.

Shooting a good score

It can be truly frightening to think about, worry about, and stress about shooting a good score. This is one fear that we should erase right now. It doesn't matter what you shoot. The question is, did you have fun? Oh, ...sorry. Never mind.

At last Peck finished his round.

In the locker room his friend Ted asked,

"How in the world did you shoot a score of 212 strokes today?"

"Well," sighed Peck,

"I missed a putt on the 18th for a 211."

The End

So you made it this far, and you are still breathing? Well, that's a good sign. That last dash through the fear chapter is sometimes hard to get through without a friend nearby. You have been through the look, the language, the basics, and those dreaded fears, but you are still hanging in there, and that is to be commended. I can do that. "I commend you!" Feel better? Good.

To finish up this book on how to handle this game called golf, I have included a few last minute tips. These should help you navigate that nasty venture you are embarking on. Have fun and don't forget that..........................what was I saying?

Last minute tips

Wear clean underwear to the course, in case you are in an accident.

Think long and hard about.........................tennis.

Don't eat yellow snow.

Remember, this is just a game.

Have fun.

Keep your head down, your shoulders square, your knees bent, your weight even, your chin up, your left arm straight, your backswing slow, your head steady, your muscles relaxed and your mind clear. Yeah, right.

Well, it looks like you made it through the golfing jungle just fine. I know that it was a long, hard trip, but I was with you the whole way, well, except for that little problem I had in the pot, and between the lines, and with death and such. Anyway, always remember that Golf is an adventure. It is fun, it is exciting and it will kick you in the head if you give it half a chance. From the readings I get from my map, you are about done with this book. Don't forget who helped you get through it. Sport and I have crossed bogs, climbed mountains, swam rivers, been boiled in grasshopper spit, and were forced to dance with my Aunt Evie. Living on the fringe is not for everyone, but you have to like it, if you are going to be a golfer. That reminds me of the time in the hills of Jaga when I played golf with Chief Jefferica. It was a tough match and of course my life was on the line. Well just then...............
.........sorry. Got carried away again. Good job pilgrim. You made it. I'm off to recover Sport, and dive into another quest for the meaning of golf. Chow!

The End, Amen

Well, that's it folks. You made it through this mind-boggling test of golf. Playing should come easy after this. I hope you enjoyed this book, and more importantly, I hope you bought a copy for your brother-in-law. But, seriously, not that I can be serious, I hope you love this great game and treat it with respect and care. It is the greatest game in the world, and I can't wait to get back to the course. Watch for more fun golf projects from Sporting Thoughts in the future.

Brule MacDuff